Fact Finders®

CAUSE AND EFFECT: AMERICAN INDIAN HISTORY

Forced Removal

CAUSES AND EFFECTS of the Trail of Tears

BY HEATHER E. SCHWARTZ

Consultant:
Brett Barker, PhD
Associate Professor of History
University of Wisconsin–Marathon County

CAPSTONE PRESS
a capstone imprint

Fact Finders Books are published by Capstone Press,
1710 Roe Crest Drive, North Mankato, Minnesota 56003
www.capstonepub.com

Library of Congress Cataloging-in-Publication Data
Schwartz, Heather E.
Forced removal: causes and effects of the Trail of Tears / by Heather E. Schwartz.
pages cm.—(Fact finders. Cause and effect: American Indian history)
Includes bibliographical references and index.
Summary: "Explains the Trail of Tears, including its chronology, causes, and lasting effects"—
Provided by publisher.
Audience: Grades 4-6.
ISBN 978-1-4914-2036-2 (library binding)
ISBN 978-1-4914-2211-3 (paperback)
ISBN 978-1-4914-2226-7 (ebook PDF)
1. Cherokee Indians—Relocation—Juvenile literature. 2. Cherokee Indians—Government
relations—Juvenile literature. 3. Cherokee Indians—History—Juvenile literature. I. Title.
II. Title: Causes and effects of the Trail of Tears.
E99.C5S369 2015
323.1197'557—dc23   2014035622

Editorial Credits
Catherine Neitge, editor; Bobbie Nuytten, designer; Eric Gohl, media researcher;
Morgan Walters, production specialist

Photo Credits
Alamy: Nativestock.com/Marilyn Angel Wynn, 28–29, North Wind Picture Archives, 11;
Bridgeman Images: © Look and Learn/Private Collection, 5; Corbis: National Geographic
Society, 21; CriaImages.com: Jay Robert Nash Collection, cover, 24–25; Getty Images: *The
Denver Post*/Al Moldvay, 22, Hulton Archive, 6, MPI, 9; Guthrie Studios: John Guthrie, 26;
The Granger Collection, NYC: 19; Library of Congress: 10, 13, 15, 16, 27

Design Elements: Shutterstock

Printed in Canada.
102014   008478FRS15

Table of Contents

FORCED REMOVAL

White Americans and American Indians shared land in the New World for centuries. Over several hundred years they'd learned to live together in settled states east of the Mississippi River.

But in 1830 U.S. President Andrew Jackson made a decision. Members of the Cherokee, Chickasaw, Choctaw, Creek, and Seminole tribes would be removed from their homes in the Southeast. Their land in Alabama, Florida, Georgia, Mississippi, and Tennessee would be given to white Americans instead.

Why couldn't the two groups continue living side by side? What caused the president's decision to forcibly move the American Indians? For the Cherokee, the move was so painful and deadly, it became known as the Trail of Tears.

Those who survived the forced move called it *Nunna daul Isunyi*—the Trail Where They Cried. Today it is called the Trail of Tears.

What Caused the TRAIL OF TEARS?

American Indians lived peacefully in the Southeast for many years before being forced from their homes.

The Trail of Tears describes the forced journey of more than 16,000 Cherokee to Indian Territory in present-day Oklahoma. But the events leading up to that brutal 1838 march began years before.

Cause #1: Huge Cultural Differences

White Americans viewed American Indians as too different. Many tribes put women in charge of farming instead of men. Indian men were busy hunting and involved in **diplomacy** and war. American Indians spoke languages other than English. They worshipped their own gods. They wore unfamiliar clothing.

White Americans couldn't accept these differences. The U.S. government wanted Indians to fit in better by behaving more like white Americans.

In the 1790s President George Washington introduced the "plan of civilization" for Indians. It focused on changing American Indian **culture**. Missionaries set up schools, where they taught Indian children English and Christianity. They divided labor at the schools the way white families did. Girls cooked, cleaned, and gardened. Boys plowed fields and chopped wood.

Adult American Indians were expected to live like white people too. Women were expected to give up farming for sewing, cooking, and other household duties. Men were expected to give up hunting and become farmers.

A Way to Survive

Some American Indians began living like white settlers as a way to keep peace. It was also a way to deal with the pressures placed on them by whites. Some wealthier American Indian families began to live like rich white Americans. Cherokee John Ross, who became chief of the tribe in 1828, lived in an elegant home on a large plantation. He grew cotton, corn, wheat, peaches, and apples. Like some white Americans of his time, he owned several African-American slaves.

diplomacy—skill in handling affairs without causing hostility or conflict (often between nations)
culture—a people's way of life, ideas, art, customs, and traditions

Cause #2: A Growing Country

As the United States grew, the demand for space to farm and settle grew too. White settlers knew the land east of the Mississippi River was valuable for growing crops and mining.

Establishing American Indians as farmers rather than hunters was an important element of the Indian "civilization plan." Farming required much less land than hunting did. So once Indians were farmers, white settlers could claim that Indians needed less land. Settlers could demand the extra land be given to whites. Most Indian peoples had no desire to change the way they had lived for generations.

American Indians didn't want to leave their homes and their **ancestral** land. But many white settlers were willing to do anything to take it. They took over land, set fires, and stole livestock to show Indians they weren't welcome and to drive them away. Still, Indians struggled to stay.

ancestral—relating to or developed from an ancestor, who is a family member who lived a long time ago

Swiss artist Karl Bodmer painted a Choctaw camp in 1833.

HISTORY OF LOSSES

By the 1800s native tribes had a history of being forced to give up land to the United States.

1814
The Creek lost 22 million acres (9 million hectares) in Georgia and Alabama after battling the United States.

1815

1818
The Seminole lost land in Spanish Florida as punishment for harboring fugitive slaves.

1818
The Chickasaw lost land in Kentucky and Tennessee.

1820

1830
The Choctaw lost more than 10 million acres (4 million hectares) in Mississippi and Alabama.

1830

Cause #3: Georgia Wanted the Cherokee Gone

By 1828 Georgia laws stripped the Cherokee of their rights and allowed the state to take their land. When the tribe tried to fight back in 1831, the U.S. Supreme Court said it did not have the legal authority to rule in the matter. That meant the Georgia laws were allowed to stand.

The Cherokee tried again in 1832. This time the Supreme Court ruled in their favor. Chief Justice John Marshall said that states could not regulate Indian land. Only the federal government had the power to pass laws affecting the Cherokee.

But victory in court didn't help the Cherokee. When Georgia ignored the ruling, Jackson looked the other way. The president refused to stop the state from continuing to take Cherokee land.

John Marshall served as chief justice of the Supreme Court for 34 years, the longest in history.

THE CASE

OF

THE CHEROKEE NATION

against

THE STATE OF GEORGIA:

ARGUED AND DETERMINED AT

THE SUPREME COURT OF THE UNITED STATES,

JANUARY TERM 1831.

WITH

AN APPENDIX,

Containing the Opinion of Chancellor Kent on the Case; the Treaties between the United States and the Cherokee Indians; the Act of Congress of 1802, entitled 'An Act to regulate intercourse with the Indian tribes, &c.'; and the Laws of Georgia relative to the country occupied by the Cherokee Indians, within the boundary of that State.

═══════

BY RICHARD PETERS,

COUNSELLOR AT LAW.

═══════

Philadelphia:

JOHN GRIGG, 9 NORTH FOURTH STREET.

1831.

The Cherokee took their case to the Supreme Court in 1831 and 1832.

Cause #4: The Indian Removal Act

While state and federal governments failed to protect American Indians' rights, Jackson took even stronger action. He supported white Americans in their quest to take over Indian land.

Jackson told Congress in 1829 that he needed authority to remove all Indians living east of the Mississippi. In response, Congress passed the Indian Removal Act of 1830, and Jackson signed it. The new law authorized him to negotiate treaties with tribes including the Cherokee, Chickasaw, Choctaw, Creek, and Seminole. In the treaties the tribes would give up their land east of the Mississippi River. The land was in what today are large parts of Alabama, Florida, Georgia, Mississippi, and Tennessee. In exchange they would be given money and granted land west of the Mississippi River, in Indian Territory.

The Indian Removal Act would give the president power to move about 100,000 American Indians from their homes on ancestral land to faraway unsettled territory.

Andrew Jackson

Even before he was president, Andrew Jackson was strongly in favor of Indian removal. As a commander in the U.S. military, he fought and defeated the Creek in 1814. Between 1814 and 1824, he helped negotiate nine treaties in which tribes gave up land to the United States. He served as the nation's seventh president from 1829 to 1837.

Andrew Jackson served two terms as president.

Tribes Had No Choice

The aim of the Indian Removal Act was to encourage American Indians to move to unsettled territory. There they could govern themselves away from white settlers.

The act said that American Indians were not to be forced into signing agreements they didn't want to make. But in reality the government gave them no choice. Negotiations didn't go so smoothly. Some American Indians signed **treaties** because they felt they had no other choice. Others resisted and were forced out. Each tribe reacted differently.

None of the tribes made an easy transition from East to West. Disagreements within the tribes over the best thing to do would divide tribes for decades.

treaty—an official agreement between two or more groups or countries

The Second Seminole War lasted until 1842, when many Seminole were sent west to reservations.

The Second Seminole War began in late 1835 when the Seminole fought the United States for their right to stay in Florida.

The Treaty of New Echota

A small number of Cherokee signed a removal treaty in their capital of New Echota, Georgia, in 1835. Under the treaty the U.S. government promised the Cherokee land in the West. It also promised them $5 million for their land east of the Mississippi River. The treaty was backed by a group led by Cherokee leader Major Ridge, his son John, and newspaper editor Elias Boudinot. They felt the situation was hopeless, and the only way to survive was to sign the treaty and move to Indian Territory.

But a much larger number of Cherokee wanted to keep fighting for their land. Cherokee chief John Ross led a petition drive against the treaty with 16,000 Cherokee signatures.

Major Ridge's Cherokee name was Kah-nung-da-tla-geh. It means "the man who walks on the mountaintop."

Even after the U.S. Senate **ratified** the Treaty of New Echota in 1836 by one vote, Ross kept fighting against it. But the government ignored him. The Cherokee were given two years to leave their land in the East. They were never paid.

ratify—to formally approve

INDIAN REMOVAL TREATIES

1830
The Choctaw sign the Treaty of Dancing Rabbit Creek; they agree to give up land in Mississippi and move to land in Indian Territory.

1830

1832
The Seminole sign the Treaty of Payne's Landing; they agree to leave Florida for land west of the Mississippi River.

1832

1834
The Chickasaw sign the Treaty of Washington; they agree to leave Mississippi for Indian Territory.

1834

MILITARY ACTION

Of the 18,000 Cherokee living in the Southeast, only about 2,000 had voluntarily left their land by 1838. It was up to the new U.S. president, elected in 1836, to deal with the remaining Cherokee. Martin Van Buren's solution meant military action.

President Van Buren sent 7,000 soldiers to round up the Cherokee in May 1838. Entire families were arrested. They were ordered from their homes at **bayonet** point. They were supposed to receive food and supplies from the government, but most did not. Many were not even allowed to gather their belongings and needed supplies. They left home with only the clothes they were wearing.

As the Cherokee were dragged away, some white settlers tried to stop the soldiers from mistreating them. Others stole from the now-empty homes, while their former owners looked on.

The Cherokee couldn't protect their homes or fight back in any way. They could only go where the soldiers forced them to go.

bayonet—a blade attached to the end of a rifle

Still in North Carolina

The Oconaluftee Cherokee of North Carolina managed to stay. About 1,000 Cherokee from Tennessee and North Carolina escaped the roundup. They eventually set up a tribal government in Cherokee, North Carolina. They became the Eastern Band of Cherokee Indians.

A wood engraving of the Cherokee's forced removal appeared in a textbook about 12 years after the roundup.

Prisoners Without a Crime

Many of the Cherokee were taken to **stockades** where they were treated as prisoners. Guards mistreated them. They didn't have enough food to eat or water to drink. They didn't have a roof over their heads to shelter them from rain and wind.

Soon the mud was several inches deep. Crowded, unsanitary conditions led to widespread illness. **Dysentery**, measles, and whooping cough spread among the tribe. An estimated 2,500 people died waiting for the roundup to be completed. Still, the men were urged to march 12 to 15 miles (19 to 24 kilometers) each day, in preparation for the journey west.

U.S. troops led the first group of Cherokee on their forced **migration** in June 1838. The summer was known as the "sickly season." Many became ill with cholera, smallpox, malaria, and dysentery. Many died.

Those left behind asked to stay until fall, when conditions for travel might be better. They wanted to remove themselves rather than being forced by troops.

stockade—an enclosure made of posts or logs set upright in the ground
dysentery—a serious infection of the intestines that can be deadly; dysentery is often caused by drinking contaminated water
migration—movement of people from one area to another

Thousands died before and during the forced removal of the Cherokee.

On the Trail of Tears

The remaining Cherokee got their wish. Their migration was delayed. It didn't make their journey any easier, though. In late 1838 they left for the West. Some traveled by river. Most walked, and many were barefoot. The winter grew icy and bitter. They struggled to cross the frozen Mississippi River. Along the way they also battled drought, disease, hunger, and exhaustion.

Marching through rain and cold was especially difficult and dangerous for the very young and the very old. Children saw their grandparents collapse to the ground. Parents carried children dead of disease and starvation. Men, women, and children wailed and cried for all of their losses.

The work of Francis (Blackbear) Bosin, an artist of Kiowa-Comanche heritage, depicted the despair of the Trail of Tears.

The journey took about six months. Those who survived had traveled about 800 miles (1,287 km) to their new land in the West. Historians believe that about 4,500 Cherokee died on the trail, which was about one-quarter of the Cherokee Nation.

The Trail of Tears

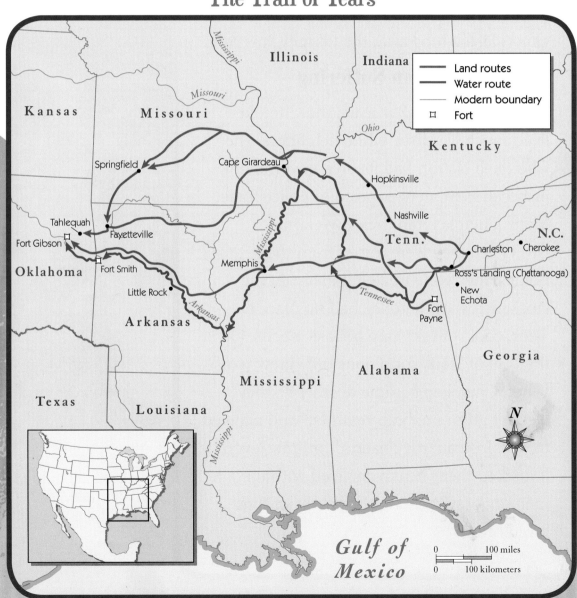

What Effects Did the TRAIL OF TEARS HAVE?

The Trail of Tears dramatically changed the lives of those forced to follow it. Its effects lasted long after the journey was over.

Effect #1: Human Suffering

Before the Trail of Tears, the Cherokee lived much like their white neighbors. The Cherokee Nation had its own government, justice system, newspaper, and police force. Many Cherokee ran their own farms.

When they were forced from their homes, they were treated harshly. In the stockades, the Cherokee had no place to sleep, cook, or take care of basic needs. On the Trail of Tears, conditions only grew worse. When Cherokee became deathly ill, they weren't given medical treatment and allowed to rest. Instead, they had to continue, even if it killed them. Survivors lived with the memory of witnessing the deaths of their loved ones.

The effects of the tragic Trail of Tears continue today.

25

Effect #2: A Divided Tribe

When the Trail of Tears ended, the Cherokee had to start over. As individuals they had lost their homes and in many cases, their family members. As a tribe they had lost their identity. For many years they had been divided on whether to follow the white settlers' way of life. Some believed it was wrong to give up traditions. The Treaty of New Echota further divided them. Some agreed with the treaty but many did not.

Ravens rip apart a Cherokee Nation scarf in artist John Guthrie's symbolic painting.

Once they reached Indian Territory, the leaders who had signed the treaty were murdered by other Cherokee. More violence followed as each side took revenge. Strong leadership was needed, but the Cherokee were also divided about how to govern. Those who had settled in Oklahoma earlier had a system in place. The new arrivals wanted a government more like the one they had before they left home.

John Ross suffered a personal tragedy on the Trail of Tears. His wife, Quatie, died after giving her only blanket to a sick child.

FAST FACT

John Ross was elected principal chief of the Cherokee Nation in 1828. He was elected principal chief of the new Cherokee Nation in 1839. He remained chief until his death in 1866. Tahlequah, in present-day Oklahoma, was the new nation's capital.

Effect #3: Struggle to Survive

The entire tribe had to work together to survive. The Cherokee Nation adopted a new constitution in 1839. The tribe built government buildings and started a newspaper. White missionaries opened schools. The Cherokee **prospered** with good soil for farming and a strong government in place.

They remained divided on many issues, however, including how white culture influenced tribal traditions.

In addition, the U.S. government continued to take away their land and their rights. Indian Territory would no longer exist. It became the state of Oklahoma in 1907.

Young women pose in front of their boarding school in the 1880s. The first Cherokee Female Seminary burned and was replaced with a new one. Today the Cherokee Heritage Center stands on the grounds of the original near Tahlequah, Oklahoma.

prosper—to do very well

Cause and Effect

When the United States took land from the Cherokee, the government wanted space for the country to grow. The United States expanded to become the country it is today. The Trail of Tears, however, is a terrible reminder of how this practice damaged the Cherokee. Despite the harsh treatment, the Cherokee survived to rebuild their own strong nation within the United States.

GLOSSARY

ancestral (an-SES-tral)—relating to or developed from an ancestor, who is a family member who lived a long time ago

bayonet (BAY-uh-net)—a metal blade attached to the end of a rifle

culture (KUHL-chuhr)—a people's way of life, ideas, art, customs, and traditions

diplomacy (di-PLOH-muh-see)—skill in handling affairs without causing hostility or conflict (often between nations)

dysentery (DI-sen-tayr-ee)—a serious infection of the intestines that can be deadly; dysentery is often caused by drinking contaminated water

migration (mye-GRAY-shuhn)—movement of people from one area to another

prosper (PROSS-pur)—to do very well

ratify (RAT-uh-fye)—to formally approve

stockade (stock-AYD)—an enclosure made of posts or logs set upright in the ground

treaty (TREE-tee)—an official agreement between two or more groups or countries

READ MORE

Benoit, Peter. *The Trail of Tears*. New York: Children's Press, 2012.

Bjornlund, Lydia. *Trail of Tears: The Relocation of the Cherokee Nation*. American History. Detroit: Lucent Books, 2010.

Bruchac, Joseph. *On This Long Journey: The Journal of Jesse Smoke, a Cherokee Boy, the Trail of Tears, 1838*. My Name is America. New York: Scholastic Paperbacks, 2014.

INTERNET SITES

FactHound offers a safe, fun way to find Internet sites related to this book. All of the sites on FactHound have been researched by our staff.

Here's all you do:

Visit *www.facthound.com*

Type in this code: 9781491420362

 Super-cool stuff! Check out projects, games and lots more at **www.capstonekids.com**

CRITICAL THINKING USING THE COMMON CORE

1. Consider Andrew Jackson's background before he was elected president. What do you think Americans wanted when they voted him into office? Use details from the text to support your answer. (Key Ideas and Details)

2. Even before the Trail of Tears, the Cherokee were divided on the issue of adopting white ways. Some felt it was a good idea; others worried more about losing traditions. Explain each side's position. (Key Ideas and Details)

3. Throughout history and even today, powerful governments have mistreated cultural groups. Can you think of any other people who were forced from their homes like the Cherokee were? (Integration of Knowledge and Ideas)

INDEX